PRINCEWILL LAGANG

The Role of Gratitude in Relationship Satisfaction

First published by PRINCEWILL LAGANG 2023

Copyright © 2023 by Princewill Lagang

All rights reserved. No part of this publication may be reproduced, stored or transmitted in any form or by any means, electronic, mechanical, photocopying, recording, scanning, or otherwise without written permission from the publisher. It is illegal to copy this book, post it to a website, or distribute it by any other means without permission.

Princewill Lagang asserts the moral right to be identified as the author of this work.

First edition

This book was professionally typeset on Reedsy.
Find out more at reedsy.com

Contents

1 Introduction — 1
2 Gratitude Defined — 3
3 The Science of Gratitude — 6
4 The Gratitude-Relationship Connection — 9
5 Expressing Appreciation — 12
6 Cultivating a Grateful Mindset — 15
7 Gratitude Amid Challenges — 18
8 Mindful Gratitude Practices — 21
9 Building Trust and Connection through Gratitude — 24
10 Nurturing Emotional Intimacy through Gratitude — 27
11 Shared Gratitude Rituals — 30
12 Reflection and Continued Growth — 33

1

Introduction

In a world bustling with technological advancements and ever-changing social dynamics, the fabric of relationships has often been tested. Amidst this whirlwind, one constant has emerged as a potential driving force behind enduring and satisfying relationships: gratitude. This book delves into the profound influence that gratitude wields on relationship satisfaction, unraveling its layers to reveal the transformative power it holds within partnerships.

At the heart of human connection lies the intricate dance of emotions and expectations. Relationships, be they romantic, familial, or platonic, are an intricate web of mutual interactions that mold our daily lives. This book is a journey into exploring how gratitude, a seemingly simple and yet multifaceted emotion, can act as a catalyst for nurturing and enhancing these vital connections.

The decision to delve into gratitude within the context of relationships is a response to the yearning for authentic connections in today's fast-paced world. Technology has provided us with unparalleled means of communication, yet it has also inadvertently distanced us from the very essence of human connection. It is against this backdrop that the exploration of gratitude becomes imperative.

Gratitude, a sentiment as old as human existence itself, has long been extolled for its psychological and physiological benefits. But its role within the realm of relationships is often overshadowed by more ostentatious emotions. In the chapters to follow, we will unveil the layers of this emotion, investigating how its expression and recognition can sow the seeds of contentment, intimacy, and longevity in relationships.

The significance of recognizing and expressing gratitude within partnerships is profound. It transcends the surface and reaches deep into the core of human interaction. As we journey through this book, we will uncover the science behind gratitude, delving into its impact on our brains, emotions, and overall well-being. Through real-life anecdotes, psychological insights, and practical exercises, we will learn how gratitude can transform the landscape of our relationships.

This book is an invitation to embrace a fresh perspective on relationships – one that transcends the traditional boundaries of give and take. It beckons us to reflect on our interactions and appreciate the subtle moments that often go unnoticed. It calls for a conscious effort to infuse our relationships with a sense of appreciation that goes beyond words, seeping into the very fabric of our behavior and intentions.

As we embark on this journey, let us keep in mind that the pages ahead are not just about the theoretical exploration of an emotion. They are an exploration of the potential that lies within each of us to foster connections that withstand the tests of time. So, let us turn the page and venture into the world of gratitude, where relationships are not just shaped by destiny, but also by our deliberate choices to acknowledge and celebrate the beauty of the connections we share.

2

Gratitude Defined

At the heart of our exploration lies the intricate emotion of gratitude, a concept that goes beyond mere thankfulness and encompasses a profound array of emotional and psychological implications. In this chapter, we will delve into the multifaceted nature of gratitude, unraveling its core components and its capacity to elicit positive transformations within individuals and relationships.

Defining Gratitude:

Gratitude can be understood as more than just the act of saying "thank you" or acknowledging a favor received. It is a complex emotional response that emerges from the recognition of the kindness, thoughtfulness, or positive actions of others. This recognition goes beyond a perfunctory acknowledgment; it involves a deep sense of appreciation and an understanding of the effort or intention behind the action.

Emotional and Psychological Implications:

Gratitude's impact stretches far beyond its surface expression. At its essence, gratitude is intertwined with positive emotions, such as joy, contentment, and warmth. When individuals experience gratitude, it often leads to a sense of emotional well-being and connection. Psychological research has shown that practicing gratitude can lead to improvements in mood, increased life satisfaction, and a reduction in stress and depressive symptoms.

Gratitude's Expansion of Positive Emotions:

Gratitude possesses the remarkable ability to expand and amplify positive emotions. When we engage with gratitude, it acts as a gateway to a range of positive feelings. These emotions include not only happiness and contentment, but also compassion, empathy, and kindness. Gratitude serves as a catalyst, setting off a chain reaction of positive affect that ripples through our interactions and relationships.

Beyond Thankfulness:

While thankfulness is an integral part of gratitude, the concept goes beyond the act of expressing thanks. Gratitude involves a deeper level of engagement with our feelings and thoughts. It encourages us to reflect on the positive aspects of our lives, shifting our focus from what is lacking to what is present. This shift in perspective can be transformative, influencing how we perceive our interactions, experiences, and relationships.

Fostering Positive Emotions:

Gratitude operates as a catalyst that not only enhances our individual emotional well-being but also enriches our relationships. When gratitude is present in interactions, it fosters positivity and enhances the overall emotional tone. It encourages individuals to recognize the efforts and intentions of others, thereby cultivating a sense of connection and mutual appreciation.

In the chapters that follow, we will explore the intricate ways in which gratitude intertwines with the dynamics of relationships. Through real-life stories, scientific findings, and practical exercises, we will uncover how gratitude, as an emotion and a practice, has the potential to shape the course of relationships, infusing them with depth, understanding, and positivity.

As we proceed, let us bear in mind that gratitude is not a standalone emotion; it is a foundational thread in the fabric of human connection. It offers us a lens through which we can observe and appreciate the nuances of our relationships, ultimately leading us towards more fulfilling and meaningful interactions.

3

The Science of Gratitude

In the previous chapter, we delved into the intricate dimensions of gratitude, understanding it as a complex emotion that extends beyond mere thankfulness. In this chapter, we take a deep dive into the scientific foundations of gratitude, uncovering the psychological studies that underscore its remarkable benefits and exploring how practicing gratitude can lead to enhanced well-being and healthier relationships.

Psychological Studies on Gratitude:

Numerous studies within the field of psychology have illuminated the transformative effects of practicing gratitude. Research consistently shows that individuals who engage in regular gratitude exercises experience a range of positive outcomes. These studies often involve participants keeping gratitude journals, where they record things they are thankful for on a daily basis.

Benefits of Practicing Gratitude:

1. Improved Mood: Engaging in gratitude practices has been linked to

improved mood and increased levels of happiness. Expressing gratitude stimulates the brain's reward pathways, leading to the release of dopamine, a neurotransmitter associated with pleasure and positive emotions.

2. Enhanced Life Satisfaction: Individuals who consciously cultivate gratitude tend to report higher levels of life satisfaction. By focusing on the positive aspects of their lives, they are better equipped to navigate challenges and setbacks with resilience.

3. Stress Reduction: Gratitude has been found to reduce stress levels by shifting individuals' attention away from negative experiences and stressors. It helps create a buffer against the negative effects of stress, promoting emotional well-being.

4. Boosted Resilience: Regularly practicing gratitude can contribute to greater emotional resilience. It encourages individuals to reframe their perspectives and find meaning even in difficult situations.

Gratitude and Relationship Health:

The impact of gratitude extends beyond individual well-being; it deeply influences the dynamics of relationships. Couples and partners who express and acknowledge gratitude toward one another often experience enhanced relationship satisfaction.

1. Fostering Connection: Gratitude acts as a bridge, connecting individuals emotionally. When partners express gratitude for each other's efforts and contributions, it reinforces the sense of being valued and appreciated.

2. Enhancing Communication: Gratitude can improve communication patterns within relationships. Individuals who express gratitude tend to be more open and empathetic, leading to healthier communication dynamics.

3. Strengthening Trust: Regular expressions of gratitude contribute to the establishment and maintenance of trust. When partners consistently recognize each other's positive intentions, it builds a foundation of mutual respect and trust.

4. Sustaining Intimacy: Gratitude enhances emotional intimacy by allowing partners to share vulnerable feelings and experiences. This willingness to express gratitude for the small moments of connection deepens the bond between individuals.

As we navigate through this chapter, it becomes evident that gratitude is not just a philosophical concept; it has a tangible impact on our psychological well-being and the health of our relationships. The science of gratitude underscores its potential as a tool for personal growth and connection. By understanding the neurobiological mechanisms that underlie gratitude's effects, we gain insights into how we can harness its power to enhance our lives and relationships.

In the upcoming chapters, we will explore practical strategies and exercises that enable us to integrate gratitude into our daily lives and relationships. The journey ahead is an exploration of how this powerful emotion can be consciously cultivated to create a positive ripple effect in our lives and the lives of those around us.

4

The Gratitude-Relationship Connection

In our quest to understand the profound impact of gratitude, we now turn our attention to the intricate relationship between gratitude and the satisfaction of human connections. This chapter delves into the ways in which practicing gratitude can elevate communication, strengthen connections, and deepen intimacy within relationships.

The Link Between Gratitude and Relationship Satisfaction:

Gratitude is like a nourishing rain that nurtures the soil of relationships. Research has consistently revealed a strong positive correlation between practicing gratitude and overall relationship satisfaction. Partners who actively express and receive gratitude tend to experience higher levels of contentment and fulfillment in their relationships.

Enhancing Communication:

Effective communication forms the bedrock of any healthy relationship, and gratitude plays a pivotal role in this realm. When individuals practice gratitude, they are more likely to engage in open and meaningful conversations. Expressing appreciation for the efforts and qualities of a partner creates an environment of affirmation, which in turn fosters more honest and empathetic communication.

Strengthening Connection:

Gratitude acts as a bridge that connects hearts and minds. When partners express gratitude for each other's actions, it reinforces the bond between them. This connection is not solely based on material gestures; even expressing gratitude for emotional support, understanding, or shared experiences can deepen the sense of companionship and unity.

Deepening Intimacy:

Intimacy thrives in an atmosphere of emotional safety and vulnerability. Gratitude facilitates this by allowing individuals to express their true feelings and experiences. Sharing moments of gratitude for the small, intimate aspects of a relationship, such as shared laughter or quiet moments, fosters a deeper emotional connection.

Building a Culture of Appreciation:

Practicing gratitude within a relationship cultivates a culture of appreciation. Partners become attuned to each other's efforts and strengths, leading to a virtuous cycle of mutual admiration. This culture acts as a buffer during challenging times, helping couples navigate conflicts with empathy and understanding.

Savoring Shared Experiences:

Gratitude encourages individuals to savor and appreciate the present moment. Partners who practice gratitude are more likely to derive joy from shared experiences, whether it's a romantic dinner or a simple walk in the park.

THE GRATITUDE-RELATIONSHIP CONNECTION

These shared moments become cherished memories that contribute to the fabric of the relationship.

As we delve deeper into the connection between gratitude and relationships, it becomes evident that gratitude is not just a fleeting sentiment; it is a practice that shapes the very foundation of our connections. By acknowledging the positive aspects of our relationships and expressing our appreciation, we create an environment of positivity, understanding, and mutual respect.

In the upcoming chapters, we will explore practical exercises and strategies that can help us integrate gratitude into our relationships. The journey ahead is a transformative one, offering us the tools to infuse our connections with a newfound sense of warmth, depth, and harmony.

5

Expressing Appreciation

In the intricate tapestry of relationships, expressing gratitude is the vibrant thread that weaves moments of connection, understanding, and warmth. This chapter delves into the art of expressing appreciation within relationships, exploring the myriad ways in which gratitude can be communicated, both through words and actions.

Verbal Expressions of Gratitude:

1. Sincere Thank You: The simplest and most direct way to express gratitude is through a heartfelt thank you. This basic acknowledgment communicates appreciation for actions, gestures, or qualities that contribute to the relationship.

2. Compliments: Offering genuine compliments is a powerful way to express gratitude. Complimenting your partner's efforts, strengths, and qualities not only conveys appreciation but also boosts their self-esteem.

3. Active Listening: Being an attentive listener is an indirect but impactful way to express gratitude. Show genuine interest in your partner's thoughts

and feelings, which communicates that you value their perspectives.

4. Words of Affection: Using affectionate language and endearing terms can express gratitude and reinforce the emotional bond between partners.

Non-Verbal Expressions of Gratitude:

1. Physical Touch: A warm hug, a gentle touch, or holding hands can convey gratitude and a deep sense of connection without the need for words.

2. Acts of Service: Taking on a task or responsibility to lighten your partner's load can be a tangible way to express gratitude for their efforts.

3. Gifts: Thoughtful gifts, whether small tokens of appreciation or grand gestures, can convey gratitude and show that you've been thinking about your partner's needs and desires.

4. Quality Time: Spending quality time together, engaging in activities you both enjoy, is a powerful way to express gratitude. It communicates that you value the shared moments.

Celebrating Milestones:

Acknowledging milestones, both big and small, is an opportunity to express gratitude for the journey you've taken together. Celebrate achievements, anniversaries, and shared experiences to reflect on your growth as a couple.

Expressing Gratitude for Emotional Support:

Sometimes, the most profound expressions of gratitude stem from acknowledging emotional support. Sharing vulnerabilities, expressing gratitude for being a confidant, and valuing the emotional safety within the relationship are ways to show appreciation.

Mindful Appreciation:

Practicing mindfulness in relationships means being fully present and appreciative of each moment. Engage in activities mindfully, and express gratitude for the shared experiences.

Customizing Expressions:

It's important to recognize that everyone experiences and expresses gratitude differently. Understanding your partner's preferences and love language can help you tailor your expressions of appreciation in ways that resonate deeply.

As we navigate through the various methods of expressing gratitude, remember that the key lies in authenticity and consistency. Expressing gratitude shouldn't be confined to special occasions; it should be an integral part of daily interactions. By cultivating a habit of appreciation, we not only enhance the overall atmosphere of the relationship but also create a space where both partners feel valued, cherished, and truly seen.

In the next chapter, we will explore ways to overcome challenges that might hinder the practice of gratitude within relationships. The journey toward nurturing gratitude is not without its hurdles, but with insight and dedication, we can overcome them to create lasting bonds enriched by appreciation.

6

Cultivating a Grateful Mindset

In the pursuit of nurturing gratitude within relationships, the journey begins with cultivating a grateful mindset in our daily lives. This chapter explores the practice of fostering gratitude as a way of thinking and being, and delves into how positive thinking can significantly impact the dynamics and well-being of our relationships.

The Practice of Cultivating Gratitude:

1. Gratitude Journaling: Dedicate a few minutes each day to jot down things you're grateful for. This practice helps shift your focus towards the positive aspects of life, no matter how small.

2. Morning Reflection: Begin your day by mentally listing a few things you appreciate. This sets a positive tone for the day ahead and encourages you to seek out moments of gratitude.

3. Mindful Presence: Engage fully in the present moment and appreciate the beauty around you. Whether it's a quiet sunrise, a shared laugh, or the aroma of a home-cooked meal, these moments are opportunities for gratitude.

4. Acts of Kindness: Engage in acts of kindness for others, even small ones. This practice not only benefits those you're helping but also amplifies your sense of gratitude for the ability to make a positive impact.

Positive Thinking and Relationship Impact:

1. Enhanced Perspective: Positive thinking allows you to view challenges as opportunities for growth rather than obstacles. This perspective shift can positively impact how you approach conflicts within your relationship.

2. Resilience and Problem-Solving: A grateful mindset fosters resilience, enabling you to navigate relationship challenges with a more constructive outlook. It encourages problem-solving and seeking solutions rather than dwelling on problems.

3. Attraction of Positivity: Positive thinking is contagious. When partners maintain an optimistic and grateful mindset, it creates an atmosphere of positivity that influences both individuals.

4. Emotional Well-Being: Cultivating gratitude improves emotional well-being by reducing stress and increasing overall happiness. Partners with a positive outlook are better equipped to handle the ups and downs of relationships.

5. Deeper Connections: A grateful mindset encourages individuals to seek out the positive aspects of their partners and relationships. This deepens the emotional connection and helps partners truly appreciate each other.

Overcoming Negativity Bias:

Human brains are wired to focus on negative experiences as a survival mechanism. Overcoming this negativity bias requires conscious effort. Regularly practicing gratitude helps rewire your brain to focus more on the positive aspects of life and relationships.

Creating a Grateful Environment:

Cultivating a grateful mindset within a relationship requires both partners to participate. When both individuals actively engage in positive thinking and express gratitude, they contribute to an environment that is conducive to love, growth, and mutual support.

As we journey through the cultivation of a grateful mindset, let's remember that it's an ongoing practice, much like tending to a garden. By nurturing a mindset that seeks out the silver linings and acknowledges the blessings in life, we pave the way for enriching relationships that are nurtured by positivity, resilience, and a shared sense of appreciation.

7

Gratitude Amid Challenges

Life is a tapestry woven with both joyous moments and trials that test our resolve. Nurturing gratitude during challenging times is a skill that not only strengthens our emotional well-being but also fortifies the bonds within our relationships. In this chapter, we explore how gratitude can be sustained in the face of adversity and discuss strategies for finding silver linings even when life presents its most trying moments.

The Resilience of Gratitude:

1. Acknowledging Struggles: Gratitude doesn't dismiss challenges; rather, it allows us to acknowledge them while seeking moments of positivity within them.

2. Balancing Emotions: While it's natural to feel a range of emotions during tough times, gratitude provides a counterbalance by helping us focus on what remains positive.

Strategies for Finding Silver Linings:

GRATITUDE AMID CHALLENGES

1. Practice Self-Compassion: Treat yourself with kindness during difficult times. Focus on the strengths and qualities that have helped you navigate challenges before.

2. Focus on Growth: Embrace challenges as opportunities for growth. By viewing them as stepping stones toward personal and relationship development, you can find meaning even in tough situations.

3. Shift Perspective: Consider challenging situations from different angles. This can reveal unexpected silver linings and provide a fresh perspective.

4. Gratitude in Small Moments: Amid adversity, appreciate the small, everyday moments that bring joy. These moments can serve as reminders of the good that still exists.

5. Seek Support: Lean on your support system, including your partner. Express gratitude for their presence and help, and allow their support to lift you up.

Mindful Gratitude in Tough Times:

1. Moment-to-Moment Awareness: Practice mindfulness by staying present in each moment. Focus on what you can control and the positive aspects of the current situation.

2. Acceptance of Imperfection: Life is full of ups and downs. Embracing the imperfections and challenges contributes to a sense of acceptance and gratitude for the journey.

Sustaining Gratitude within Relationships:

1. Open Communication: During challenging times, openly communicate with your partner about your feelings, concerns, and gratitude for their

support.

2. Shared Reflection: Reflect on the journey you've taken as a couple and express gratitude for the strength you've built together.

3. Collective Coping: Approach challenges as a team. Working together to overcome obstacles fosters unity and reinforces gratitude for the partnership.

The Power of Perspective:

Gratitude in the face of adversity is a testament to the power of perspective. While challenges may cloud the landscape temporarily, gratitude acts as a beacon, illuminating the positive aspects that persist even in difficult times. By nurturing gratitude amid challenges, we cultivate a deep sense of resilience, both within ourselves and within our relationships.

In the next chapter, we will explore how gratitude can be integrated into various types of relationships – from romantic partnerships to family connections and friendships. The principles of gratitude are universal, and by applying them, we can enrich the tapestry of every relationship we hold dear.

8

Mindful Gratitude Practices

The art of mindful gratitude invites us to immerse ourselves fully in the present moment, cultivating an awareness that deepens our connection to the world around us. In this chapter, we explore the concept of mindfulness and its profound role in enhancing gratitude within relationships. We also delve into mindfulness exercises that can contribute to heightened relationship satisfaction and a more profound sense of appreciation.

Understanding Mindfulness:

Mindfulness is the practice of being fully present and engaged in each moment without judgment. It involves directing our attention to our thoughts, feelings, and surroundings with an open and accepting mindset. Mindfulness allows us to experience life without being preoccupied by the past or anxious about the future.

Mindful Gratitude and Relationships:

1. Present-Centered Connection: Mindfulness enhances our capacity to

be fully present with our loved ones. This presence fosters a deep sense of connection as we listen, understand, and engage with intention.

2. Amplifying Gratitude: Mindfulness magnifies our ability to appreciate the small and meaningful moments in relationships. By being fully engaged in the present, we can recognize and celebrate the positive aspects of our connections.

Mindful Gratitude Exercises:

1. Mindful Breathing: Set aside a few minutes each day to focus on your breath. As you inhale and exhale, let go of distractions and tune into the sensation of breathing. This practice helps ground you in the present moment, making space for gratitude.

2. Gratitude Walk: During a walk, pay attention to the sights, sounds, and sensations around you. As you do, reflect on aspects of your relationships that you're grateful for, whether it's a partner's support or shared experiences.

3. Mindful Listening: Engage in conversations mindfully by fully listening to your partner. Put aside distractions and truly absorb their words, fostering deeper understanding and connection.

4. Body Scan Meditation: Practice a body scan meditation, moving your attention through different parts of your body. Use this opportunity to express gratitude for your body's abilities and the moments of connection it allows.

5. Three Good Things: At the end of each day, reflect on three positive aspects of your relationships or interactions. Write them down and savor the positive emotions associated with them.

6. Mindful Eating: During meals, eat slowly and savor each bite. As you do,

express gratitude for the nourishment, the company you're sharing, and the effort that went into preparing the meal.

Mindful Conflict Resolution:

Even during conflicts, mindfulness can play a transformative role. Engage in mindful breathing before addressing conflicts, allowing you to approach the conversation with a calm and open mindset. This practice can prevent heated arguments and facilitate more productive conversations.

By integrating mindfulness into gratitude practices, we infuse our relationships with a profound depth of presence and appreciation. The practices outlined in this chapter offer a gateway to heightened awareness, fostering an environment where gratitude flourishes and relationships thrive. In the concluding chapter, we'll reflect on the journey of exploring gratitude within relationships and offer a vision for the enduring impact of these practices.

9

Building Trust and Connection through Gratitude

In the symphony of human relationships, trust and emotional connection are the harmonious notes that resonate deeply. Gratitude emerges as the conductor that orchestrates these elements, weaving a tapestry of intimacy and security. This chapter explores the profound ways in which gratitude plays a pivotal role in cultivating trust and forging emotional connections, while also delving into the transformative effects of appreciating each other's efforts in fostering a sense of profound security within relationships.

Gratitude as the Weaving Thread of Trust:

1. Acknowledgment of Intent: When partners express gratitude for each other's actions, it's a testament to their mutual recognition of positive intentions. This acknowledgment of motives nurtures trust by demonstrating an understanding of one another's motivations.

2. Vulnerability and Trust: Gratitude encourages vulnerability by allowing

partners to openly express appreciation. This vulnerability cultivates deeper emotional connections, nurturing trust through shared openness.

A Bridge of Emotional Connection:

1. Shared Moments: Gratitude often arises from shared experiences and meaningful interactions. These shared moments serve as bridges, connecting partners on a profound emotional level and fortifying trust.

2. Empathy and Understanding: The practice of gratitude prompts partners to empathize with each other's feelings and perspectives. This deepened understanding fosters emotional connections and strengthens the trust between them.

The Power of Appreciation for Security:

1. Feeling Valued: Expressing gratitude regularly conveys a consistent message of being valued and cherished. This feeling of being treasured contributes to a bedrock of security within the relationship.

2. Creating Emotional Safety: Gratitude establishes an environment of emotional safety, wherein partners feel comfortable expressing themselves without fear of judgment. This emotional safety forms the cornerstone of trust.

A Positive Loop of Gratitude and Trust:

1. Mutually Reinforcing: Trust and gratitude create a virtuous cycle. As trust deepens, partners are more inclined to express gratitude. Simultaneously, expressing gratitude reinforces the sense of trust.

2. Navigating Challenges: The trust nurtured through gratitude provides a buffer during challenges. Partners with strong trust are more likely to

collaborate in overcoming difficulties and navigating uncertainties.

Gratitude: A Source of Connection and Joy:

1. Shared Positivity: Gratitude directs partners' attention to the positive facets of the relationship. This shared positivity enhances the emotional connection, generating moments of happiness and fulfillment.

2. Communal Growth: Expressing gratitude for the journey of growth and shared experiences strengthens the commitment to mutual development. This celebration further deepens the connection between partners.

As this chapter concludes, it's clear that gratitude acts as both architect and sustainer of trust and emotional connections. Its capacity to recognize and celebrate each other's efforts, intentions, and shared experiences lays the foundation for an environment of empathy, security, and appreciation. Through our exploration of gratitude's impact on relationships, we uncover its transformative capacity to create bonds that weather adversity, celebrate growth, and resonate with joy.

10

Nurturing Emotional Intimacy through Gratitude

Within the sacred chambers of relationships, emotional intimacy thrives as a beacon of connection and understanding. Gratitude emerges as the gentle gardener of this intimacy, tending to its growth with care. In this chapter, we delve into the profound impact of gratitude on enhancing emotional intimacy, while also exploring the intricate relationship between vulnerability, open communication, and the practice of gratitude.

The Dance of Gratitude and Emotional Intimacy:

1. Recognition of Vulnerabilities: Gratitude encourages partners to recognize and appreciate each other's vulnerabilities. This recognition forms the basis of emotional intimacy, as it demonstrates a willingness to truly see and value each other.

2. Deepening the Emotional Bond: Expressing gratitude for shared moments and emotional support deepens the emotional bond between partners. This

shared appreciation forms the bridge to understanding and closeness.

The Role of Vulnerability:

1. Shared Openness: Vulnerability and gratitude are intertwined. The act of expressing gratitude often involves opening up about feelings and emotions, which nurtures a sense of vulnerability and emotional connection.

2. Mutual Trust: Vulnerability is built on trust, and gratitude paves the way for this trust to flourish. When partners openly express gratitude for each other's efforts, it reinforces a sense of security, fostering deeper vulnerability.

Open Communication as an Expression of Gratitude:

1. Honest Expression: Gratitude thrives in an atmosphere of open communication. Partners who engage in transparent conversations about their feelings and needs are better equipped to express appreciation and understand each other.

2. Sharing Inner Worlds: Open communication is an avenue to share one's inner thoughts and feelings. This sharing, when coupled with gratitude, enhances emotional intimacy by revealing the depth of emotions and thoughts.

Appreciating Vulnerabilities:

1. Acknowledgment of Efforts: Expressing gratitude for the efforts made by partners to open up emotionally nurtures a sense of safety. This acknowledgment encourages a willingness to be vulnerable, further enriching emotional intimacy.

2. Empathy and Validation: Gratitude for shared vulnerabilities validates partners' feelings and experiences. This validation contributes to a deep sense

of connection, where partners feel truly understood and accepted.

A Sanctuary of Emotional Intimacy:

1. Creating a Safe Space: Gratitude fosters an environment where partners feel safe to be their authentic selves. This sense of safety encourages the sharing of thoughts, feelings, and vulnerabilities.

2. Shared Moments of Gratitude: Moments of expressing gratitude for emotional support and understanding strengthen the emotional bond. These moments serve as anchors of emotional intimacy within the relationship.

As this chapter concludes, it's evident that gratitude serves as a luminous guide on the path to nurturing emotional intimacy. Its capacity to foster vulnerability, open communication, and mutual appreciation nurtures a sense of connection that transcends words. Through our exploration of gratitude's role in relationships, we unveil its transformative ability to create spaces where partners can truly connect on a profound emotional level, celebrating each other's vulnerabilities and fostering a rich tapestry of emotional intimacy.

11

Shared Gratitude Rituals

Just as constellations light up the night sky, shared gratitude rituals illuminate the landscape of relationships with their gentle glow. This chapter delves into the concept of weaving gratitude rituals into the fabric of relationships, exploring the transformative power of practices such as gratitude journals, nightly reflections, and shared appreciations. These rituals act as the bridge that connects partners on a profound level of appreciation, understanding, and connection.

Incorporating Gratitude Rituals:

1. Creating Sacred Spaces: Introducing gratitude rituals carves out sacred spaces within relationships where partners come together to reflect, appreciate, and connect.

2. Rituals as Nourishment: Just as nourishing food fuels the body, gratitude rituals provide nourishment for emotional connections. Regular engagement in these rituals sustains the emotional well-being of partners.

The Gratitude Journal:

SHARED GRATITUDE RITUALS

1. Reflection and Writing: Keeping a gratitude journal encourages partners to reflect on daily experiences and identify moments of appreciation. Writing down these moments solidifies the positive emotions associated with them.

2. Sharing and Connection: Partners can periodically share entries from their gratitude journals, offering a glimpse into their inner thoughts and fostering a deeper connection.

Nightly Reflections:

1. Daily Highlights: Before sleep, partners can reflect on the day's highlights and express gratitude for moments that brought joy, love, or growth.

2. Mindful Recap: Engaging in mindful nightly reflections shifts the focus from daily stressors to moments of positivity, allowing partners to end the day on a positive note.

Shared Appreciations:

1. Appreciation Exchange: Partners can set aside dedicated time to verbally express appreciation for each other. This can include acknowledging each other's efforts, qualities, and shared experiences.

2. Creative Expression: Partners can engage in creative ways of expressing gratitude, such as writing each other appreciation notes, creating art, or planning surprise gestures.

The Ripple Effect:

1. Positive Atmosphere: Gratitude rituals infuse relationships with positivity, creating an atmosphere where appreciation is a constant presence.

2. Cultivation of Habits: As gratitude rituals become habits, they cultivate

a mindset of appreciation that extends beyond the rituals themselves, permeating everyday interactions.

The Journey of Shared Gratitude:

1. Connection through Practice: Engaging in shared gratitude rituals deepens the emotional connection between partners. The act of expressing and witnessing appreciation creates bonds of understanding and unity.

2. A Lifelong Voyage: The exploration of shared gratitude rituals is an ongoing journey. As partners grow and evolve, these rituals evolve with them, constantly renewing the spirit of appreciation.

In conclusion, shared gratitude rituals transform relationships into sanctuaries of appreciation. By incorporating practices like gratitude journals, nightly reflections, and shared appreciations, partners infuse their connections with a sense of intention, reflection, and heartfelt acknowledgment. As we journey through the exploration of gratitude within relationships, these rituals stand as beacons of connection, reminding us of the profound impact that appreciation has on shaping the tapestry of our connections.

12

Reflection and Continued Growth

As we draw near to the culmination of our exploration, it's time to reflect on the transformative journey of incorporating gratitude into relationships. This chapter serves as a space for introspection, summarizing key takeaways, and offering guidance for maintaining a gratitude-centered approach that enriches the tapestry of connections and fosters enduring growth.

Reflecting on the Journey:

1. Embracing Awareness: Reflect on how your awareness of gratitude has evolved throughout this journey. Recognize the moments where gratitude has touched your relationships, both in subtle and profound ways.

2. Growth and Transformation: Consider how practicing gratitude has influenced your own personal growth and the growth of your relationships. Reflect on the shifts in perspectives, habits, and emotional connections.

Key Takeaways:

THE ROLE OF GRATITUDE IN RELATIONSHIP SATISFACTION

1. Power of Appreciation: Gratitude is a potent force that nurtures emotional bonds, encourages vulnerability, and fosters trust and emotional intimacy.

2. Mindful Connection: Incorporating mindfulness into gratitude practices amplifies the depth of connections by grounding them in the present moment.

3. Resilience Amid Challenges: Gratitude acts as a resilient shield during challenging times, allowing partners to navigate difficulties with empathy and support.

Guidance for Continued Growth:

1. Integrate Gratitude into Daily Life: Continue to integrate gratitude practices into your daily routine. Whether through journaling, shared appreciations, or reflections, make appreciation a habit.

2. Celebrate Milestones: Reflect on your journey and celebrate milestones in your relationship's growth. Use these moments to express gratitude for the shared experiences.

3. Open Communication: Maintain open communication with your partner about the impact of gratitude. Share your insights, experiences, and the positive changes you've noticed.

4. Adapt and Evolve: Relationships evolve, and so should your gratitude practices. Stay attuned to each other's preferences and explore new ways of expressing appreciation.

5. Model Gratitude for Others: Extend the practice of gratitude beyond your primary relationships. Model gratitude for friends, family, and colleagues, creating a ripple effect of positivity.

A Journey Unfolds:

REFLECTION AND CONTINUED GROWTH

As you reflect on the chapters that have unfolded, remember that the journey of gratitude within relationships is one that unfolds continuously. Just as a garden needs ongoing care to flourish, relationships thrive with constant attention and nurturing. The practice of gratitude serves as a compass, guiding you toward the heart of connections, enriching your interactions with understanding, empathy, and appreciation.

With each chapter, you've delved deeper into the intricacies of gratitude's impact on relationships. Now, armed with insights, practices, and a renewed sense of purpose, you stand at the threshold of an enriched journey ahead. May the tapestry of your relationships continue to be woven with threads of gratitude, nurturing bonds that are resilient, joyful, and ever-evolving.

www.ingramcontent.com/pod-product-compliance
Lightning Source LLC
LaVergne TN
LVHW020459080526
838202LV00057B/6052